This be returned on or before

D1448093

STIRLING DISTRICT LIBRARIES

3 8048 00321 7119

English Silver

COLLECTORS' BLUE BOOKS

English Silver

JESSIE McNAB DENNIS

STIRLING
DISTRICT
LIBRARY

STUDIO VISTA, LONDON

For T.E.D.

739.23

DEN

Page 1: FIG. 1   Chamber candlestick. London, 1710. Maker: Augustine Courtauld. 6¾ in. wide. The Metropolitan Museum of Art, New York, Bequest of Mary Strong Shattuck, 1935.

FRONTISPIECE: Ewer. London, 1700. Maker: David Willaume. 8 in. high. Victoria and Albert Museum, London.

Opposite: FIG. 2   Tankard with design reserved against a finely matted ground. London, 1646. Maker's mark, a bird with a branch. 4⅛ in. high. Collection of Irwin Untermyer.

Copyright © 1970 by Jessie McNab Dennis

All rights reserved. No part of this book may be reproduced or transmitted in any form or by any means, electronic or mechanical, including photocopying, recording or by any information storage and retrieval system, without permission in writing from the Publisher.

SBN 289 36944 4

Published in London 1970 by Studio Vista Ltd, Blue Star House, Highgate Hill, London N19

Printed in the United States of America
Jacket designed by the Bert Clarke Design Group

I A Royal Cup

BOUND TO OBEY—BOUND TO OBEY AND TO SERVE—BOUND TO OBEY. These
three declarations were prominent features in the design of a jeweled gold cup
made to the order of Henry VIII as a gift to his queen, Jane Seymour. According to a royal inventory, the cup weighed "three score and five ounces and a
half" and was melted down in the Netherlands at the order of a later king, the
unfortunate Charles I. The drawing for it (FIG. 3), prepared by Hans Holbein
in 1536, fortunately still survives as a memento of the king's only happy mar-
riage—happy not only in the romantic sense but also dynastically, for Jane
produced Henry's only male heir, the future boy-king Edward VI.

Henry VIII was the first English sovereign to have a "modern" education.
In contemporary terms this meant that he had undergone the versatile training
of a Renaissance prince and was as familiar with music, classical literature and
art as with military matters and affairs of state. It is no coincidence that the
Renaissance, which had already penetrated from Italy to Germany and France,
finally arrived in England early in Henry's reign. In the very year of his accession, 1509, he invited the Florentine Pietro Torrigiano to come to England to
design the tombs of his father, Henry VII, and Margaret Beaufort, his paternal
grandmother. Further commissions were soon given by the king and the
nobility to other Italians as well as to French, Netherlandish and German
artists who could work in the Renaissance manner. The German Hans Holbein came to England for the first time in 1526. He is best remembered as a
painter and miniaturist, but he also made drawings for the guidance of goldsmiths that were thoroughly Renaissance in design.

Queen Jane's cup therefore is of more than sentimental interest. The form
itself was German in origin, but became popular in England and was appropri-
ately known as a "thistle cup" from the shape of the bowl, which resembles in
outline a thistle flower. The bowl is supported by an elaborate stem rising

FIG. 3 A cup for Jane Seymour. Design by Hans Holbein, ca. 1536. Courtesy the
Ashmolean Museum, Oxford.

from a stepped spreading base; the cover repeats the proportions of the base and is surmounted by a tall finial. The decoration indicated for the cup is a very compendium of all those motifs, foreign to England and her goldsmiths, which constituted the Italian decorative style. These motifs had been re-covered from Italy's own historic art of a millennium and a half earlier, when they usually had some mythological significance. The winged cherubs (Erotes) who hold up the empty shield destined to be engraved with the queen's arms; the fish-tailed Nereids who blow long, curving horns and incidentally support the middle section of the finial; the open-snouted dolphins bracketing the middle section of the stem; the disembodied heads of a cherub, a satyr and several rams all are classical in origin (the last-mentioned originally alluding to an actual animal sacrifice). The vegetable and abstract ornament was also de-rived from the antique world: ubiquitous acanthus leaves, swags of laurel, and three slightly different patterns of gadrooning on the base, the cup and the cover. But the band of interlacing arabesque ornament at the top of the cup, just below the cover, was of Eastern and more recent origin. This type of deco-ration was absorbed into Italian ornament through her Eastern contacts and was taken over in the northern countries as part and parcel of the Italian Renaissance style. Around the middle of the bowl were four roundels contain-ing heads of kings and queens in relief. The embellishment of the cup was completed with pointed and table-cut diamonds, pearls, and the repeating linked initials of Henry and Jane highlighted in polished gold against a matte ground.

An object such as Queen Jane's cup naturally represented the very latest ideal in court taste. The Renaissance style, however, was no passing fashion, and as the sixteenth century progressed, font-shaped silver cups and silver-mounted wooden mazers, which had been the standard drinking vessels of the well-to-do, were made in diminishing numbers. In their place the newer Ger-man covered cups—such as the thistle cup and others suggestive of gourds and melons—were preferred, and Gothic ornament gave way to that of Italian derivation. Such decoration was not, of course, confined to drinking cups but was applied to all objects made by the goldsmiths.

The general acceptance of German forms and Renaissance decoration was undoubtedly partly eased by the presence in London of a number of German goldsmiths, working in their own idiom, while the importation of Augsburg- and Nürnberg-made plate reinforced their influence. Engraved pattern books

and design sheets printed commercially in Germany, Italy and the Netherlands, with the intention of acquainting goldsmiths with the newest styles,
were also readily available in London so that the adoption of Renaissance
motifs presented, in fact, no insuperable problems to the native London goldsmiths. They had been trained in an ancient tradition, and their technical
knowledge was equal to the demands of the new fashion.

FIG. 4   Goldsmiths' Row, Cheapside, 1547. Detail from a watercolor of the coronation procession of Edward VI. The Society of Antiquaries of London.

FIG. 5   Silver-gilt cylindrical salt. London, 1584–1585. Maker unknown. 11⅜ in. high. The Metropolitan Museum of Art, New York, Gift of Chester D. Tripp, 1952.

II The London Goldsmith

OF ALL THE TECHNICAL ARTS, that of the goldsmith was England's noblest. Archeological discoveries give evidence of a continuous tradition of goldsmithing from a period at least as remote as the late Bronze Age; for more recent periods written sources record the fame of English work. A school of Anglo-Saxon goldsmiths was established in the ninth century at the Holy See in Rome, and in the Middle Ages work "in the English manner" was highly prized all over Europe. By the middle of the eleventh century a vast store of objects in silver and gold had accumulated in the English abbeys and monasteries and England's new Norman overlords "gazed in wonder" (according to William of Poitiers, the historian) both at the abundance of precious metals and at the intricacy of their workmanship. Much of this treasure was plundered and carried back to Normandy. In the following century the large ransom raised to liberate Richard Coeur de Lion from imprisonment in Austria was partly collected from precious vessels also surrendered by the Church. But these were only the earliest of a series of vandalisms committed from various motives, which removed the palpable evidence of much of the glory of English goldsmithing. London, from this time, became the principal center of the practice of the goldsmith's art.

Large amounts of wrought gold and silver would seem to have been made in the thirteenth century, but the Black Death in the fourteenth century—the single most devastating event in all English history—and the protracted civil wars in the fifteenth century gave little opportunity for the survival of a continuous body of the work of the medieval goldsmith. Until the sixteenth century, by far the greatest patron had been the Church, since silver and gold objects not only were required for liturgical use (according to canon law) and the decoration of shrines, but also for the domestic use of the thousands of clerics and other religious living in convents and monasteries. The dissolution of the monasteries and thoroughgoing spoliation of all Church property ordered by Henry VIII swept into the melting pot, therefore, most of the remaining silver and gold made since the Norman Conquest. The melting pot also claimed a large part of the secular silver made between the reigns of Henry VIII and Charles I. As a means of procuring bullion it was used by both sides in the civil war of 1642-1652. The Royalist and Parliamentarian armies obtained funds through the melting down of voluntary (and involuntary) levies of the domestic and corporate plate of their supporters.

Individuals have also played a not inconsiderable part in the destruction of old plate. In the sixteenth century a very great deal of medieval domestic plate was exchanged for work in the latest Renaissance fashion and this has undoubtedly been the response to every succeeding style introduced in silver. Quite apart from fashion, however, is the purely monetary consideration. Ever since 1238 English law has required that wrought silver should be of the "sterling standard," that is, of the standard of purity made originally by the "Esterlings," those German miners and refiners whose skills were employed all over Europe in the Middle Ages. Sterling had (and has) only 7½ percent copper alloy to 92½ percent fine silver. Since exactly the same standard was used for silver coinage, it is understandable that in times of financial stringency families could convert their silver wares into capital with very little trouble.

The goldsmiths' sources of supply appear to have originated principally from within the island for the whole of the early periods. They did not, of course, do their own refining, but bought the gold and silver already refined from "parters" who managed the ore-crushing and refining operations. Silver is also frequently found in conjunction with lead and had been a side product of lead mines since Roman times. The important sites for these were in North Wales, Devonshire, York and Durham. Additional quantities also became available as a result of trade with Europe, where the great mines of Austria and Hungary contributed to the principal supply. There was never much in the way of a surplus, probably, for various acts were passed in the Middle Ages forbidding the export of the gold coinage; also, gold and silver wares were not to be taken out of the country without an export license. A greater supply was generally available from the early sixteenth century on, when the European mines increased production and the Spanish control of Mexican and Peruvian mines brought vast quantities of precious metal into the Iberian peninsula, from whence, through money transactions in the normal course of trade, it was carried all through Europe. This no doubt eased the problem of supply in England both indirectly and directly, for the frankly piratical activities of the privateers, encouraged by the home government, resulted in the inflow of quantities of plundered Spanish bullion.

There was an acute shortage of silver at the end of the seventeenth century, but from the early eighteenth century on, silver production in all the established centers increased. Because of her general prosperity as a nation at this time—a prosperity that was not general in the condition of *all* the people—England was able to take full advantage of the rise in worldwide silver production. There was an ample supply both for the Mint and the goldsmiths, and the abundance and weight of eighteenth-century silver objects reflect this.

The relations between the Mint and goldsmiths have been close from a very early period. The first London goldsmith known by name, Otto the Elder (working 1090-1100), is recorded as being also "graver to the Mint," and down through the centuries various eminent London goldsmiths served as Wardens and Masters of the Mint and were regularly appointed to test the purity of the gold and silver coinage. The officers of the Mint, however, exercised no reverse control over the goldsmiths. Early Royal decrees and later Acts of Parliament allowed the goldsmiths themselves to see that legislation concerning their craft was enforced by their own elected officers.

Ever since 1327, when the London goldsmiths were allowed to form a guild, or "mystery" (from Latin *ministerium*), various factors have tended to encourage a certain homogeneity in the craft in London. A clause in a law of 1400 obliged them to have their workshops, with retail premises attached, in a single area, that known as the Cheap and the King's Exchange. The purpose of this clause was to make the task of inspection easier—for the preamble of the law mentioned that fraudulent workers using more than the allowed amount of alloy or even producing work in base metal with only a surface of silver or silver-gilt had escaped general detection because their workshops were in unfrequented areas of the city. Such proximity as necessarily resulted from this law undoubtedly made new fashions quickly known among all the practicing goldsmiths and was a factor in the establishment of new styles.

There were other organizational factors controlling the life and products of the London goldsmiths. The first of these was the system of hallmarking. By the time of Elizabeth I hallmarks consisted of four distinct symbols (right) struck in the semifinished article by the Master or Warden of the guild. Of these the "leopard's head"—a representation of a full-face lion's head—was the oldest. It had been introduced in 1300 and signified that the object so marked had been tested and found to be of the required standard of purity.

All plate made for sale had to be tested and marked in this way and the leopard's head was known as "the King's mark."

In 1363 another law was passed requiring every goldsmith to have a mark or symbol unique to himself with which objects made by him were to be struck immediately after they had been tested and marked with the King's mark. The wardens, by the same law, were instructed to keep a register of all goldsmiths' marks. The point of this law was that the maker could always be traced if a question should later arise about the quality of the ware. It was, in fact, a second check on the production of fraudulent work. The goldsmiths themselves were responsible for the introduction of the third mark, what was at first known as the "Hall mark" but is now called the "date letter." So that it might be known in precisely what year a piece of silver had been tested and found adequate, the wardens affixed a letter of the alphabet by striking it alongside the leopard's head and the maker's mark. The letters have run in cycles of twenty from 1478 to the present. Each cycle has a consistent style both of the letters and of the outline around them, which sufficiently distinguishes it from all others. The fourth mark, that of a lion passant— a lion in profile walking to the left with one forepaw raised—was introduced in 1544. The purpose of this mark is not precisely known, but since the coinage had only shortly before been debased—as a temporary measure—it is probable that it was an additional guarantee of standard, since no such debasement of the metal was allowed in wrought wares.

A further force which tended to unify the London goldsmiths was, of course, their craft guild, the Worshipful Company of Goldsmiths. This had originated in the early medieval period as a voluntary association of trade craftsmen. The association was given formal recognition by the Charter of Edward III in 1327. This Charter was several times renewed and the privileges and duties of the Company also gradually increased under succeeding pieces of legislation. By the middle of the sixteenth century the London guild was in a powerful position, for the various acts of Parliament framed with specific regard to the craft in London were explicitly stated to apply to goldsmiths working in all other parts of the kingdom. Furthermore the London guild was empowered to enforce the legislation concerning standards not only upon the London Guildsmen but also those in the provinces. Until the opening of provincial assay offices, therefore, in such important centers as Exeter, York, Chester and Norwich, all work had to be sent to London for hallmarking.

The first Goldsmiths Hall was built in 1340 on a site near St. Paul's Cathedral and the Guildhall. (The fourth building on the same site stands there today.) The goldsmiths lived in close community in the area around their Hall, for they usually lived above or behind their workshops, which by law were situated in and around Cheapside. The Hall was the center of the goldsmiths' corporate activity. It was here that they met in company for the religious feasts that were and still are observed by all the Livery Companies of London. An especially important feast was that held yearly in honor of their patron saint, St. Dunstan. He was himself a goldsmith and was reputed to have tweaked the Devil's nose with his tongs. It was through the Hall that young men entering upon an apprenticeship were bound to their Masters and the records of these contracts were deposited for safekeeping at the Hall. It was in the Hall, too, that a workshop was maintained where the apprentice seeking to register his mark at the end of his training made his "complete work, commonly called a Masterpiece to be begun and finished by himself without instruction from any." The guild also undertook the charitable work necessary for the sick, orphaned and widowed relics of its Guildsmen and the education of certain children. The charitable work in particular still continues today and so does the work of rigorously enforcing the standard of wrought wares. The Trial of the Pyx, a traditional but not meaningless ceremony, also still continues. Each year specimens of the nation's coinage are brought in a Pyx (a special round box) and are assayed by members of the guild in the presence of the King's Remembrancer and the Chancellor of the Exchequer.

As London outgrew its old city walls and spread westward, especially after the Great Fire of 1666, goldsmiths also moved their premises into the newly expanding areas of St. James and Soho. The Hall, however, remained on its ancient site and continued to be of central importance.

Many goldsmiths became outstanding in the larger sphere of London life. Sir Martin Bowes was a working goldsmith who not only filled the office of Warden of the company but was also twice Lord Mayor of London and Master of the King's Moneys. He had the great honor of serving wine, in the office of "botteler," to Queen Elizabeth at her coronation. Sir Hugh Myddleton, a crony of Sir Walter Raleigh, was also a goldsmith, but engaged in other enterprises. He undertook to divert the New River from Ware to Islington, a village to the north of the city, and thus produced a new source of water that is still in use today. Because many goldsmiths kept reserve stocks of silver and coinage on their premises, they naturally had the opportunity to turn banker. Some of the earliest banks in the city had their beginnings with the "running-cashes" of seventeenth-century goldsmiths, many of the earliest bankers being prominent members of the Company. Sir Francis Child ultimately gave up goldsmithing completely and founded Child's Bank with Robert Blanchard. He became Lord Mayor of London in 1698. Other goldsmith-bankers were Sir Hugh Myddleton, already mentioned, Sir Thomas Vyner, Sir Robert Vyner, Alderman Blackwell and Sir Richard Hoare, who founded Hoare's Bank.

The calling of goldsmith was always one of great prestige, but, of course, there were many goldsmiths with very much smaller establishments. Some, such as the spoon makers, might work alone. Others might have one or more journeymen—trained workers hired by the master.

It was illegal to operate as a goldsmith without being a member of the guild. Admission depended on the applicant's having served a thorough apprenticeship to a master goldsmith, and the payment of an entrance fee. The arrival at mastership through serving an apprenticeship was, of course, common in all the technical trades and crafts of Europe. In England, however, the terms governing the legal contract between the master and the pupil and the duties and responsibilities of each party were not codified in the form of law until early in the reign of Queen Elizabeth, in 1564. By this law apprentices served seven years and spent most of their teens "learning by doing" under the eye of a practicing goldsmith. Thus ancient methods of working the precious metals were passed along from generation to generation, methods that could interpret in these unique materials any decorative style that came into general fashion. Let us therefore examine the processes that were in use in the workshops of the London goldsmiths in the sixteenth century.

The term "workshop" rather than "studio" is used deliberately. Except in one-man enterprises that were severely limited as to quantity and character of wares that could be made, finished products of the goldsmith's art were the result of various cooperative efforts and the place of work was busy and rather noisy, with different kinds of skilled work all going on at the same time.

The master goldsmith bought silver and gold in a pure state from the refiner. The process of melting the metals and adding the legal percentage of alloy was undertaken in the workshop, where a fire constantly burned. The alloyed molten metal was poured into molds of roughly brick shape and allowed to cool into solid ingots. These were transformed into sheet silver by a worker

COLOR PLATE I   Chinese Blue and White Ming porcelain ewer with English silver-gilt mounts. London, 1590. Maker's mark, three trefoils voided in a shaped shield. 13⅝ in. high. The Metropolitan Museum of Art, New York, Rogers Fund, 1944.

Above: FIG. 7   Engraved work (detail of Figure 17).
Below: FIG. 8   Pictorial engraving (detail of Figure 20). The wide, dark areas prob-
ably made by the scorper, the fine lines cut with the graver.
Opposite: FIG. 6   Flat-chasing and extremely fine matting (detail of Figure 39).

wielding an immense hammer. Frequent annealings were necessary, since the pounding of the hammer, though gradually spreading and flattening the silver, also reduced the natural malleability of the metal. Under continued hammering it would ultimately crack, but before this stage was reached the silver was set into the fire until glowing a cherry red, then taken out and immediately plunged into a tank of cool water. This process, called "annealing," restored the malleability of the silver. The task of reducing the cake of silver continued in this way, now by hammering, now by annealing, until a large sheet was produced. Silver to be wrought into wares was then cut out from this sheet.

Hollow wares started as a mere disk of sheet silver. The center point was found with a pair of compasses and a little depression struck there with a steel punch. The compasses were also used to find the positions of eight equidistant radial lines that were marked between the edge of the disk and a circular line delineating the area of the base. The disk was then crimped along these lines: taking a wooden mallet with pointed edge, the goldsmith or one of his journeymen hammered along each line, holding it against a special narrow-armed anvil provided with a channel down the middle. The mallet forced the silver into this channel, and when done eight times there were eight crimps in the disk, raising it into an open dishlike form with walls at an angle of about thirty degrees or a little less from the level of the base. The dish was next supported from the inside over another special anvil called a "stake," and submitted to many circuits of the raising hammer. A variety of stakes, each with a different curvature, was available in every workshop, and by a judicious choice of stake and the patient application of the raising hammer the rudimentary vessel could be pressed up into any previously planned shape, whether one with vertical sides, or having a shaped profile. Each time the raising hammer had gone over the vessel one circuit from top to bottom, it had to be annealed.

When the vessel had received its destined shape, much work remained to be done before it could be called a finished piece. The marks of the raising hammer were removed by the application of the planishing hammer. This was a round, slightly dome-headed tool that was taken several times all over the surface of the vessel, which was supported from the inside, as in the raising process, by a stake of suitable curvature. Intermediate annealings, as before, were frequent. The brightly polished surface was the result of further careful and patient processes. First the outer walls of the vessel were filed to remove any remaining inequalities, then further smoothed inside and out with pumice stone and water. The minute scratches left by the pumice were rubbed away with a smooth, soft stone now known as Water of Ayr Stone or simply Ayr Stone. The outer surface was then ready for a final buffing with jeweler's rouge. Any haste or carelessness in any of these steps, or lack of understanding of the form treated, could utterly wreck the line of the ware arrived at in the raising process. For this reason the understanding cooperation of the workers was essential, and it was truly beneficial that all had undergone a similar technical training as apprentices.

There were a number of decorative techniques for the embellishment of the ware. The most obvious, of course, was the application of gold to the surface.

Gilding involved dissolving mercury in molten gold and applying the fluid amalgam to the finished vessel. It was customary to prepare the surface by roughening it slightly with a wire brush. The object was then heated in the fire where the heat drove off the mercury in the form of a noxious vapor and left the gold intimately keyed to the pores of the silver. With gilding, the medieval goldsmith often combined enameling and jewel setting to embellish important commissions, and this was indeed continued in Renaissance Italy. In the sixteenth century in England, however, commissions for the Protestant churches tended to be of the simpler kind, and Catholic ritual vessels would be made for a minority practicing their rite inconspicuously in private chapels. The broader social base for the consumption of secular plate also required a less extravagant norm. For this reason, goldsmiths had less and less occasion to make large vessels in gold, and worked more in silver, though continuing to be called "goldsmiths." Accordingly, the silver of this period relies for decoration mainly on a number of techniques carried out on the body of the ware itself. Most of these techniques had already evolved before the period when greatest reliance was placed on them.

Casting was much employed for the small sculptural accents demanded by the Renaissance style. These were not the abstract arcadings and pinnacles of the earlier period but grotesques, masks, and animal, human or mythological figures doing duty as feet, finials and handles. The molds for many stock motifs seem to have been generally available, and were probably not made anew in each workshop for every job. Other special features, however, would have been made by first forming a positive in wax and making the negative mold from it. The castings were made by running molten silver into the negatives and leaving it to cool and harden. The process of flooding the mold, usually of

FIG. 9   Repoussé work (detail of Figure 5).

quite a small scale, with the molten metal required great experience and judgement to obtain a clean casting without blemishes, such as pocking of the surface left by air bubbles. When the castings were quite hard and cold they would be neatened up with small hand tools and fixed permanently to the body of the vessel with silver solder. Filing away the visible residue of solder from around these joins was a tedious job that an apprentice might be entrusted with.

A design in relief on the wall of the vessel itself was not cast, but made by a technique called "repoussé." It was in great demand for the intricate designs of strapwork with other motifs such as swags of fruit, lion masks, and festoons of laurel leaves or drapery set symmetrically around it (FIGS. 9, 10).

The design was first drawn on the body of the vessel, which was then filled with a mixture of warm pitch mixed with brick dust. This became quite compact and firm after cooling. Working from the front with a chasing hammer and blunt tools, the design was lightly indicated as the vessel itself rested on a

FIG. 10   Underside of repoussé work (detail of Figure 5).

sawdust cushion. Then the pitch was emptied out and a higher relief gained by
pushing out the design from the inside. This was done by transferring the
impetus from a blow on one end of a hooked "snarling iron" to the other end,
which rested against the inner wall of the object. The pitch, which had to be
poured into the vessel whenever the work was continued from the outside,
supported and protected the vessel from becoming misshapen under the blows
of the chasing hammer, yet allowed the silver to yield in the specific areas
where the chasing tool was held and struck by the hammer. The process of
working first from outside then from inside continued until the design was
raised far enough, and then given final definition in front with relatively deep
channels of chasing. The repoussé technique was time-consuming and labori-
ous, yet the effect could be made in no other way. There is an observable range
of skill seen in repoussé work of the sixteenth century; sometimes it is crisp
and high, sometimes, in the hands of a less skillful or patient worker, it is flatter
and the outlines of the design are less accurate than the pattern required.

When a pattern of a linear nature was selected, two methods were available —"flat-chasing" and engraving. Flat-chasing was made by hammering a blunt tool along the lines of the design in a series of minute stuttering advances. A slight depressed groove resulted, and on thin silver a raised line was sometimes seen on the reverse of the ware. Flat-chasing was a peculiarly English technique and was especially charming in the chinoiseries of the seventeenth century that will be discussed below (FIG. 6).

The second method for linear designs was, of course, engraving, an ancient method, newly adopted in Italy in the fifteenth century and followed all over Europe in the sixteenth for carrying out many patterns suggested by commercial design sheets. These were often of an abstract nature—moresques, interlacing strapwork and scrolling tendril-and-leaf ornament. The instruments used were called "gravers" and "scorpers," both of steel, like most hand tools. Gravers are triangular or lozenge in section; scorpers are half-round or square-sectioned. The point was sharp enough to cut out a fine thread of silver from the surface, when pushed along it with the hand (no hammer was used). A minute v-shaped or curved trench thus delineated the pattern. In England a rather coarse gauge graver was used, but in the last third of the sixteenth century, when complete pictorial scenes were engraved, a finer tool was used and a few extremely cunning hands have been identified. In the eighteenth century also, much fine engraving was done, but in the main engraving was an art at which Europeans rather than the English consistently excelled (FIG. 8).

For both techniques, flat-chasing and engraving, the object was set on a thick cushioning pad, by the aid of which the work was held steady and the object itself not pressed out of shape. Hollow wares were supported from the inside with pitch; flat pieces such as trays, plates, salvers and plaques were also conveniently anchored in a shallow tray of pitch.

Various methods were available for giving the surface a non-reflecting area. Panels of "hit-and-miss" work were simple and gave a pleasing effect. Holding the area over a stake, little linear marks were made at intervals, the marks of one row being placed above the spaces between the marks of the row below and so on alternately. The method sounds tedious but it was only a case of repetition with a simple tool and hammer, and the ground was quite quickly covered. This was executed better than a kind of coarse engraved hatching that was often used in conjunction with engraved arabesques, to give the interior of the shapes outlined in engraving a matte appearance. A very fine dull effect often used to set off polished areas or work in repoussé was made with the matting tool. This was a steel rod with one of a number of possible criss-cross or mosslike designs on one end. For the finest effects, the end so prepared would be quite small, certainly never more than an eighth of an inch long and sometimes smaller. The pattern on the end of the rod was transferred to the silver by holding it against the surface, over a stake, and tapping it sharply with the chasing hammer, then moving it all over the area to be matted in a similar way. Very often there were unavoidable places where the tool had missed or not joined the preceding strike exactly, so that it was customary to take the matting tool several times over the area, until the surface was uniformly matted.

In the seventeenth century some objects were matted almost all over, as the only decoration, and this gave an interesting and not unpleasing effect when well done, though requiring little sense of art, which was necessary for engraving, chasing and repoussé. Sometimes a simple design was carried out in mat-

FIG. 11 "Hit-and-miss" work, between two areas of repoussé. From the mount of a tankard, 2nd half of the 16th century. Private collection.

ting against a polished ground, sometimes the arrangement was the reverse; the design was polished and the ground was matted. Usually the line between the two areas was delimited with a flat-chased or engraved line or with a series of coarsely engraved dashes (FIGS. 2, 12).

An interesting technique that represented a saving of labor but presented an effective decorative appearance was possibly taken in the medieval period from Continental models. It was in use in the later Middle Ages and in the earlier transition period of the sixteenth century, but it was most frequently employed in the second half of the century. This consisted of relatively narrow bands or strips of silver stamped in a steel die with a repeating pattern. These strips were usually soldered in place at the foot or rim of an object or in any collar areas, such as around the base of a finial or the boss of a stem. The patterns might be simple variations of fretted bands and classic egg-and-dart frieze design. Toward the latter part of the sixteenth century very pretty semi-pictorial designs were used, with, for instance, birds or flowers (FIG. 13). These stamped designs, though actually in relief and originally quite crisp in finish, were never in high relief, or obtrusive in any way and provided a quieter note of ornament on objects that were otherwise elaborately decorated.

The goldsmiths were not, in fact, reluctant to adopt any mechanical aid, having no notion of the romance of handwork, in an era of universal handwork in the arts and artistic crafts. Before the middle of the sixteenth century, silver wires were made laboriously at the bench with the hammer, from thin strips of cut silver. The invention of the draw-plate for drawing wires was introduced from France, and was credited to a Frenchman called Archal. By this method strips of silver were drawn through small conical holes in a steel plate, and then passed progressively through holes of diminishing size until the required gauge was reached. Wires, both full round and half round, were very useful to give strength and rigidity to hollow vessels, when soldered, for instance, around the midpoint and at the lip. They incidentally provided a molding which had a quiet decorative effect (FIG. 18).

A pretty design often seen on wine cups at the end of the sixteenth century was very simply made with a single rather broad punch. The cup had to be filled with pitch, as for engraving. Then a rod with a squared end but somewhat rounded corners was struck against it, the surface dimpling at this point. An allover beaded diaper could thus be made by striking the punch all over the surface in a predetermined order. Decoration of this type did not last long into

Above: FIG. 12 Silver-gilt wine cup, matted design within flat-chased outlines. London, 1653. Maker's mark, ET with crescent below. 3¾ in. high. Collection of Irwin Untermyer.

Below: FIG. 13 Repeating stamped flower design (detail of Figure 5).

the seventeenth century, but the punch was still used for giving a beaded effect, most often as a line of demarcation between two zones of decoration; in the later period a rather finer width of punch was used (FIG. 14).

Above: FIG. 14 Silver-gilt wine cup with allover punched diaper. London, 1599. Maker unknown. 7¼ in. high. Collection of Irwin Untermyer.

Opposite above: FIG. 15 Salver. London, 1773. Maker: John Carter. 27½ in. diameter. The Metropolitan Museum of Art, New York, Gift of James A. Moffett, 1960.

Below: FIG. 16 "Pie-crust" salver. London, 1742. Maker: probably John Swift. 18½ in. diameter. The Metropolitan Museum of Art, New York, Bequest of Ogden Livingstone Mills, 1938.

III Tudor and Early Stuart

THE ACCESSION OF ELIZABETH TUDOR to the throne of England was an auspicious event for the London goldsmiths. Although great national events marked her reign, the general policy of her ministers was one of peace and economy at home and, in foreign affairs, national security and avoidance of foreign interference. The general condition of a great part of the populace improved, and commerce, which had been a small matter in the hands of foreign merchants, assumed great proportions. The number of people who could afford to patronize the goldsmiths greatly increased and more than made up for the loss of the great patron of the Middle Ages, the Church.

In one matter, however, ecclesiastical commissions remained important and this was in the obligatory use of the communion cup at the communion service. Whereas in the Roman rite only the sacrament of bread was offered to the communicants, the sacrament of wine being reserved for the priest alone, the Protestant rite insisted that communion "in both kinds" should be offered. The substitution of the larger communion cup for the earlier chalice had been ordered during the reign of Edward VI, was set aside during the following reign, that of his Catholic sister Mary, and was again enforced during the reign of their sister Elizabeth. In parishes with large congregations the use of flagons for replenishing the communion cup was required and these offered additional chances of work for the goldsmiths. This activity naturally occupied a number of years and provided a steady stream of work for the London goldsmiths, for it was only in the larger provincial centers, such as Norwich, York, Exeter and Chester, that the local goldsmiths had the requisite skill to carry out the changeover to communion cups.

The stylistic advance from Gothic to Renaissance had already been accomplished by the time of Elizabeth's accession. Thus much of the silver of her reign has a distinctly exotic and overdecorated appearance. This was fre-

FIG. 17   Communion cup and paten. London, ca. 1560–1580. Maker unknown. 7⅞ in. high. The Metropolitan Museum of Art, New York, Rogers Fund, 1913.

quently true even of objects made for liturgical use.

Many parish churches still own their sixteenth-century communion cups. A capacious gilt one of London make, belonging to the Church of St. Michael-le-Belfrey in the city of York, dates from the actual year of Elizabeth's accession in 1558. The maker's mark is present but unfortunately cannot be identified. The decoration of the cup indicates how completely the Renaissance style had been absorbed by the London goldsmiths by the middle of the sixteenth century. Bands of interlaced ornament encircle the bowl, whereas the large baluster stem is decorated with plain repeating ovals. Lion masks in relief are set at intervals on a median rib. The paten, used for offering the sacrament of bread, is fashioned as a dish on a reel-shaped foot. Its underside and foot are decorated in conformity with that of the bowl and thus, when turned upside down, becomes a suitable cover for the cup. Many cup and paten combinations of this type were made. It is noteworthy that a number of decorative techniques, apart from the final gilding, were used on this piece. This is an unusually rich communion cup; many were quite plain, according to the size or wealth of the parish for which they were made, or they had only a band of gilt at the lip or rather sketchily engraved moresque ornament encircling the bowl. Neither the pagan origins of the more elaborate Renaissance ornament nor the infidel associations of the simpler moresque designs seem to have presented any ideological problems to the minds of either congregation or clergy in their application to these Christian sacramental vessels!

As for domestic silver we can infer from Elizabethan wills and inventories, including royal inventories, that a variety of useful objects were made in silver, including large pieces such as firedogs and andirons. We read also of silver warming pans, candlesticks, wall sconces, snuffers, toasting forks, orange strainers, scent bottles, inkstands, clocks, soapboxes, hot-water jugs and shaving bowls, but only a few examples of each have survived. Next to spoons, silver plates seem to have been the commonest and most numerous item of domestic silver made, but unlike spoons, all the plain ones have perished and only a very few of the decorated ones have been preserved (FIG. 20).

Those objects which have survived in any numbers at all are all associated with the ceremony of formal dining. Among these the large common saltcellar, the "great salt," was uniquely English. From time immemorial salt has been of immense importance to man, and in England a single large and ceremonious receptacle for it was provided as a common supply for those sitting down to-

FIG. 18   Silver-gilt communion cup and paten. London, 1558. Maker unknown. 9 in. high. Church of St. Michael-le-Belfrey, York.

gether to eat. As a central piece on the table, the salt was often of precious metal and richly decorated. In the Middle Ages the salt had usually been of hourglass shape, though descriptions of some very elaborate and whimsical ones are known, none of which have survived. In Elizabeth's time special commissions were undoubtedly given, but the standard shapes were three in number: square, cylindrical and bell-shaped.

The "great salt" was always covered and the example illustrated is no exception. The cover is surmounted with a military figure and the vessel itself rests on the backs of three little lions. The entire surface of the drum-shaped body and the cover is closely decorated with grotesque masks, swags of fruit, festoons and cartouches symmetrically arranged. A delicate repeating floral design runs around the base of the cover and another of ovolos is fixed at the foot. As with most important Elizabethan pieces, this salt is gilt all over and is decorated with a recourse to a number of techniques. The main design is carried out in repoussé with chased outlines and other details engraved. The ground is very finely matted (FIG. 5).

Above: FIG. 20 Parcel-gilt plate, engraved with *The Birth of Jacob and Esau.*
London, ca. 1550–1575. Maker unknown. 7¾ in. diameter. The Metropolitan
Museum of Art, New York, Gift of C. Ruxton Love, Jr., 1965. The "13" visible in
the border is the Strasbourg mark, possibly added in the seventeenth century.

Opposite: FIG. 19 Rare silver-gilt perfume bottle. London, 1577. Maker's mark,
IF. 4¾ in. high. Collection of Irwin Untermyer.

FIGS. 21, 22   Parcel-gilt ewer and basin. London, 1567. Maker unknown. Ewer: 13¼ in. high; basin: 19⅝ in. diameter. The Metropolitan Museum of Art, New York, Lent by C. Ruxton Love, Jr., 1948.

"Parcel-gilt" is the term for an object that is gilded in certain areas only. It represented an economy in the use of gold and at the same time afforded a pleasing color contrast between the yellow of the gilded areas and the "white" of the ungilded silver. Parcel-gilding as a decorative resource was especially favored in the Elizabethan period. It is seen on a beautiful ewer and basin of the year 1567 (FIGS. 21, 22). Ewers with basins en suite customarily contained rose water with which, on formal occasions and in great households, the diners would rinse their hands. Whether this was more of a ceremonial than a truly hygienic custom cannot now be ascertained. The custom was ultimately dropped, but a surprising number of ewers and basins can be counted among the surviving examples of sixteenth-century plate. The parcel-gilt set illustrated is further embellished with engraving of more than usual finesse and suggests the possibility of its being decorated by one of the foreign goldsmiths active in London at the time. The ewer is subtly shaped with a narrow neck and a spout cut in an arabesque line. Figures of English kings in niches are engraved around the body. The foot is lightly engraved with a beautiful continuous design of flowers and tendrils; a coarser frieze of tendrils and snails occupies the top of the body below the neck. The basin also has portraits of the English kings alternating with scenes from the Old Testament set on the border; the center has pictures of the last four Tudor sovereigns, also alternating with biblical scenes; and a battle scene decorates the boss. This scheme is so particular as to suggest that it may have been commissioned for a special occasion or person. Unfortunately, its ownership cannot be traced further back than the Hyde family in the later seventeenth century.

More is known of the second ewer illustrated, for a reliable tradition connects it with the furnishing of Burghley House in Northamptonshire, one of the country houses of William Cecil, Lord Burghley, the Lord High Treasurer of Elizabeth's reign. It came to the sale room in 1888 and was in the collection of John Pierpont Morgan for a number of years before being acquired by the Metropolitan Museum of Art in New York. The silversmith's job here was to mount a Chinese porcelain bottle and thus convert it into an object of contemporary usefulness. Since the blue of the decoration as well as the pure white of the porcelain body were equally admired—marveled at, in fact—the mounts, which are of silver-gilt, obscure as little as possible of the vessel. The bottle is supplied with a foot from which rise six narrow hinged straps shaped to the pear-shaped profile of the bottle and joining a collar at the base of the neck.

Winged cherub heads and ropes of laurel leaves decorate the straps, and a Nereid with intertwining forked tail makes a sturdy handle. All this work is done by casting, but for the repeating designs around the base of the foot, which were stamped. No attempt was made to harmonize the mounts, which are in standard Renaissance style, with the decoration of the bottle itself, which is purely Chinese. The choice of silver-gilt rather than plain silver, however, gives the wonderfully serene color scheme of blue, white and gold. The mounts were made about 1590 by an unidentified silversmith whose mark consisted of three trefoils voided in a shaped shield (COLOR PLATE 1). This mark occurs on other Chinese porcelains with English silver mounts, so the goldsmith may well have specialized in this kind of work. Porcelain was not the only rare, costly or otherwise unusual material mounted in this way, for we know of ostrich eggs and coconuts converted into drinking cups in this manner and other pieces are known with a body of such diverse materials as mother-of-pearl, Turkish pottery, reverse painted glass, serpentine, crystal, agate, German stoneware and Chinese celadon.

Handsome and heavily decorated drinking cups in the shapes of thistles, gourds or melons were made throughout Elizabeth's reign. All required their cover to be in place for the completion of the suggested shape. Such designs came originally from Germany. The native font-shaped cup, a holdover from the Middle Ages, had passed from favor altogether by about 1575, when beakers and tankards started to be generally popular—neither was a "courtly" drinking vessel (FIGS. 23, 25). Toward the end of the Elizabethan period new forms of domestic invention were introduced and existed side by side with the "naturalized" ones. They tend to be either completely undecorated or very lightly decorated with a scattering of engraved naturalistic flowers, with leaves and tendrils. The type with a bowl and cover forming together an egg shape was favored for several decades. A more short-lived type seen in the last two decades of the sixteenth century had a bowl rather resembling the pointed end of an egg—quite wide at the lip but diminishing rapidly toward the base so that it is about the same width as the last element of the baluster stem on which it is raised. The cover tends to be a flattened dome, which is then given height by a tall graduated baluster finial of several elements. The example illustrated in Figure 24 is of silver and quite undecorated except for four rosettes on the spreading stepped foot. It stands 7½ inches and has the mark of the year 1590–1591. The maker is unidentified.

Above: FIG. 23   Silver-gilt tankard. London,
1585. Maker: John Harryson. 7¾ in. high.
Collection of Irwin Untermyer.

Below: FIG. 24   Wine cup. London, 1590.
Maker unknown. 7½ in. high. Victoria and
Albert Museum, London.

Opposite: FIG. 25   Beaker with engraved
decoration. London, 1599. Maker unknown.
5¾ in. high. Collection of Irwin Untermyer.

In the reigns of James I and Charles I two new items appeared: shallow dishes with shell handles and no foot rim and small wine tasters of similar shape with elementary scrolled handles. The silver for these pieces is often remarkably thin and the scrolled handles are often simply cut from a length of wire, bent to shape and soldered on without more ado. Such vessels were made at minimum cost for the material and its decoration of simple round punches arranged in geometrical or stylized flower patterns (FIG. 26).

Plate in the early seventeenth century was fashioned in the various styles existing in the late Elizabethan period. The three pieces illustrated in Figures 27 to 29 were all made, interestingly enough, within three or four years of one another and demonstrate this point. The charming plain wine cup, 9⅜ inches high, has a bowl deriving from the egg-shaped cups already mentioned. Completely without decoration, its proportions and the various elements of the stem alone give it grace with elegance and strength with stability. This kind of cup would have been used in the households of the well-to-do. The second cup also derives from the egg-shaped cup. The finial of its cover, a three-sided

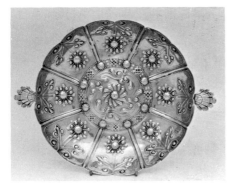

Right: FIG. 28   Steeple cup. London, 1625.
Maker: F. Terry. 17¼ in. high. Victoria
and Albert Museum, London.
Opposite left: FIG. 26   Silver-gilt dish with
punched decoration. London, 1631. Maker:
William Maundy. 7⅞ in. diameter. Collection of Irwin Untermyer.
Opposite right: FIG. 27   Wine cup. London, 1623. Maker's mark, RS and anchor.
9⅜ in. high. Victoria and Albert Museum,
London.

FIG. 29   Silver-gilt candlestick. London, 1624. Maker's mark, a trefoil in a shaped shield. 9 in. high. The Museums of the Moscow Kremlin.

pierced pyramid, names the pieces in this group. Called "steeple cups," they are a specifically English development, though steeples were also seen on plain salts. The brackets on which the pyramid is raised should be noted. Brackets also occur at the top of the steeple and as a decoration on the stem. The base rises from a stepped foot into a hollow trumpet shape; the stem itself is abbreviated and rests between two collars of stamped work. The repoussé decoration is a relaxed spaced frieze of acanthus leaves and a flower form suggestive of the Persian carnation. The ovals filled with vertical ribs are rather reminiscent of the metal purling seen on contemporary embroidery. A silver-gilt candlestick is the third object from this group. It bears the date letter for 1624–1625 and may possibly have been among the pieces of royal plate sold to Russia in 1627. The massy shape and rigid decoration in Renaissance style show it to be of an archaizing nature and possibly indicate an exhaustion of ideas for important silver for grand occasions. The advances in design seem to have been limited to less formal objects and those for personal use, such as the wine cup discussed above. The workmanship of this candlestick, which is one of a pair now in the Kremlin Museum, is nonetheless of the first quality, in spite of its dated ornament.

The location of this last piece—the Kremlin—deserves a digression in the way of explanation. Commercial contacts between England and Russia had been established in 1555, following the discovery of a North Sea route to Russia by Richard Chancellor in 1553. Large gifts of plate were made to the czar by the Muscovy Company, which for some eighty years enjoyed privileges in trading inside Russia that were not accorded to the Hamburgers and Hollanders, merchants who, using Chancellor's route, arrived on the scene only shortly after. (The last in a series of gifts of plate to the czar was made in 1663 by the Earl of Carlisle's Embassy.) The candlestick of 1624–1625 is probably not a gift but part of a group of objects from the Jewel House authorized to be sold in 1626. That year Parliament had made a totally inadequate grant for the support of the King's Majesty and ready money to make up the deficiency was raised by the sale of royal plate. The royal goldsmith, John Acton, himself bought the plate and was able to resell it to the czar through the agency of the Muscovy Company. Whether as gifts or purchases the English silver conveyed to Russia in the sixteenth and seventeenth centuries was preserved by the Romanovs and passed into state ownership at the Revolution. A large and important collection of rare Tudor and Stuart silver is thus still to be seen in cases in the Kremlin.

The use of the spoon is of great antiquity but in England was probably not widely employed until about the twelfth century, when there appears to have been a greater number made. They do not appear to have been plentiful, however, until the later Middle Ages, when the ownership of a silver spoon would be the first object of precious metal that a person in easier circumstances would acquire. (Forks were an Italian invention and were not widely used in England until the seventeenth century, although Queen Elizabeth possessed a set of twelve with agate handles—probably a gift from a foreign power.)

Elizabethan spoons show a remarkable uniformity of shape in the design of the bowls but great variety in the finish of the stem. The bowls were somewhat of a rounded triangle in outline with the narrower part joining the stem. The handles might end quite simply in pointed or acorn shapes or flat disks—all finishes that had been first used in the Middle Ages. Some specially interesting figural finials survived into the early seventeenth century. The "apostle" spoons are, of course, the best known to us. These had the figure of an apostle on the end of the stem, which was usually gilt, although this gilding has sometimes worn quite thin on extant examples. Unbroken sets of twelve spoons, each with a different figure of an apostle as a finial, are known but are now very rare. "Broken" sets survive in greater numbers and single examples are numerous. A few sets of thirteen are known, with the figure of Christ on the thirteenth spoon (FIG. 30). Saints, angels and "wode wose" (wild men) were also used and one specially commissioned set had representations of the "Twelve Heroes". Other finials were the "Maidenhead" (thought to be the head of the Virgin) and the "lion sejant" (a compact, small finial in the shape of a seated lion). The handles of these spoons were invariably straight and usually six-sided. Spoons with curved handles do not appear until the end of the seventeenth century.

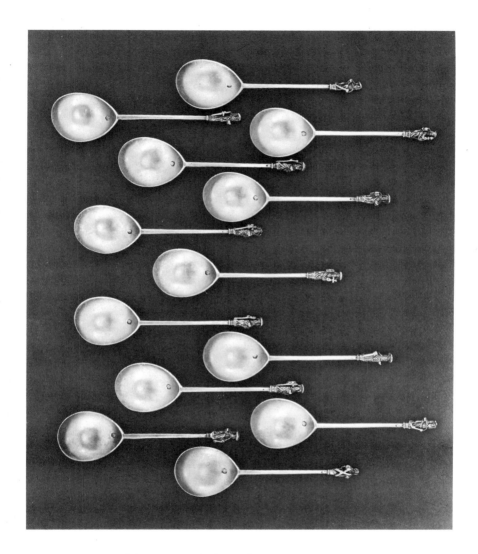

FIG. 30   Rare set of thirteen matched apostle spoons. London, 1617. Maker's mark, a crescent enclosing a star. 7¼ in. long. The leopard's head mark is struck in the bowls near the handle. The maker's mark and date letter are struck on the back of each handle. This was usual for spoons. The flat addition above each figure's head is a nimbus, and each is chased in relief with a dove, although this is not visible in the photograph. Francis E. Fowler, Jr. Collection, Los Angeles.

IV Commonwealth and Restoration

THE FIRST REPUBLICAN STATE of the modern world was neither France nor the United States, but England, whose revolution, originally over a point of constitutional reform, took place more than a century before that of the other two countries. The "Commonwealth" lasted less than a decade, and there may be some food for speculation in the idea that no regime can last long in England if it expects to suppress the theater permanently! The Puritan will to govern seems to have collapsed with the death of Oliver Cromwell, the "Lord Protector," whose son, though inheriting the position, readily stood down for the restored monarchy.

A long period of political and economic uncertainty had preceded the ten years of civil war. Eight years of official puritanism were to follow. This was altogether a lean period for the goldsmiths. Little new silver was made and there was an almost total cessation of the development of new styles. Very great amounts of privately and corporately owned silver were melted down for the support of the Royalist cause, furthermore.

During the military dictatorship of the victorious Parliamentarians, the Puritans' notorious distrust of the beautiful certainly affected the appearance of what little silver was made. Plain styles, however, had been offered by the silversmiths for some fifty years, and it is not so much the sudden appearance of undecorated silver (FIG. 33), as a certain number of rather graceless objects associated with the decade 1650–1660 that have encouraged the use of the term "Puritan" silver. The so-called "Puritan" spoon, with an oval bowl and straight flat handle (FIG. 32), had a longer vogue and was—in any case in terms of design—imported from the Continent.

It is a great pity that the reign of Charles I cannot be remembered as that of patronage for the goldsmith's art, for he was one of the few true connoisseurs of art among the English sovereigns and laid the foundation of the royal

FIG. 31 Sconce. London, 1702. Maker: John Fawdery. 9⅛ in. high. The Metropolitan Museum of Art, New York, Bequest of Mary Strong Shattuck, 1935.

collection of paintings, both by his purchases abroad and by his patronage of living artists.

The restoration of the monarchy in the person of Charles II in 1660 introduced a new period of great opportunity for the London goldsmiths. The reopening of the theaters was only one of the immediate and heady reversals of policy with the fall of the Puritan regime. Great amounts of domestic silver melted down during the civil war had to be replaced as well as silver for state and royal use, including, of course, most of the regalia for the coronation ceremony. The exuberance and largeness of proportion of silver made after the Restoration lasted until the end of the century.

The caudle-cup shown (FIG. 35) dates from the year of Charles' accession and bears the hallmark of the silversmith GS, who included a crook in the design of his punch. The particular form of two-handled cup had actually evolved from the period of Charles I, and the handles, in the form of scrolled terminal figures, had been a standby for some decades. However, the broad naturalistic flowers in repoussé, derived from Dutch models, is characteristic of the new impulses. The cap-cover has a flat disk-type finial resting on a brief spool-shaped stem that could be turned over to act as a foot when the cover was removed, rather in the way of the paten on communion cups. The chased and repoussé decoration of the plate illustrated in Figure 36 is also derived from Dutch sources: a lion and a greyhound with belled collar, both in swelling relief, chasing each other at full career around the rim among large tulips and poppies interrupted only by a contemporary coat of arms. The plate is datemarked 1677.

During the reign of Charles II silver was extravagantly used by members of the court. One reads with amazement of silver beds, large mirror frames, tables and even chairs. A certain amount of this silver furniture has survived. Some

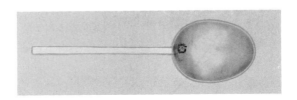

Above: FIG. 33   Tankard. London, 1656–1657. Maker's mark, HB conjoined, a star below. 4⅜ in. high. Courtesy S. J. Shrubsole, New York.

Below: FIG. 34   Trencher salt. London, 1714. Maker: Thomas Folkingham. 2¼ in. wide. The Metropolitan Museum of Art, New York, Bequest of Mary Strong Shattuck, 1935.

Opposite: FIG. 32   "Puritan" spoon. London, 1657. Maker: Stephen Venables. 4¾ in. long. Collection of Irwin Untermeyer.

Above: FIG. 35 · Silver-gilt caudle-cup. London, 1660. Maker's mark, GS, and a shepherd's crook. 6 in. high. Victoria and Albert Museum, London.

COLOR PLATE II Above: Silver-gilt loving cup. London, 1742. Maker: Paul de Lamerie. 15⅛ in. high. The Metropolitan Museum of Art, New York, Bequest of Alfred Duane Pell, 1925. Below: Silver-gilt fruit dish. London, 1766. Maker: Thomas Heming. 19⅛ in. wide. The Metropolitan Museum of Art, New York, The Jules S. Bache Collection, 1949.

of the furniture, particularly the bed said to have been used by the Duchess of Portsmouth, was undoubtedly of sheet silver laid over a wood frame, but nevertheless the quantity of silver used represented an enormous outlay of money on the metal alone, without taking into account the cost of the workmanship.

The use of silver for furnishing extended to lighting fixtures. An object that was made in great quantities was the silver wall sconce. This was fitted with one or two arms for candles, the silver wall plate forming a very satisfactory reflecting surface for the candlelight. The example illustrated (FIG. 31), although datemarked 1702, is of a form that had been in style for several decades by then. The wall sconces, though often differing in details, are of a standard general pattern and are certainly the most Baroque of the smaller silver objects of the period. The outer outline is octagonal; the candle holder projects forward on a curved arm from the lower side. The polished reflecting area is set at the center of a matte area chased with a fish-scale pattern. Each end of a pendant garland of flowers is supported in the beak of an eagle's head set one to each side, while two amors above support between them an urn and hold in their hands a fall of flowers. The owner's crest, an eagle's head pierced at the throat by an arrow, is fixed to the top of the urn. The whole sconce and its decoration in relief was made in one operation by casting (with the exception of the candle arm and reflecting plate), then worked over with hand tools for minor details. The sconces were the work of John Fawdery in 1702 or 1703.

Toilet sets for ladies' dressing tables were other extravagances of the late seventeenth century. They consisted usually of a large standing looking glass, a pair of candlesticks, many little pots and boxes and the all-important pincushion (pins themselves were handmade items that only the well-to-do could afford). The group of objects illustrated in Figure 39 is selected from a large silver-gilt toilet service of seventeen pieces made in 1683. The pictorial design is carried out in "flat-chasing," with extremely fine matte work used for shading. The decoration, an early appearance of chinoiserie, is noteworthy because it was only briefly adopted by the London silversmiths in the last two decades of the seventeenth century. Chinoiserie on London silver is always of this sketchy and artless type, whoever the maker, and suggests the objects to

FIG. 36   Plate. London, 1677. Maker unknown. 11¼ in. diameter. The Metropolitan Museum of Art, New York, Rogers Fund, 1913.
FIG. 37   Detail of Figure 36. The armorial is engraved, the flowers done with chased and repoussé work, with several textures of matted work for shading.

Above: FIG. 39   Group of silver-gilt objects from a lady's toilet service. London, 1683. Maker's mark, WF. Mirror: 22¼ in. high. The Metropolitan Museum of Art, New York, Fletcher Fund, 1963.

Opposite: FIG. 38   Standish. London, 1725. Maker: Simon Pantin. 10¾ in. long. The Metropolitan Museum of Art, New York, The Jules S. Bache Collection, 1949.

be decorated may have been farmed out for chasing to a group of specialists working in a homogeneous manner from a relatively limited number of patterns. The inspiration for this kind of decoration is to be found, of course, in the imported Chinese lacquer panels and boxes that had a contemporary vogue in furnishings.

The Restoration not only ushered in an era of extravagance at court (though it was comparable in no way to the immense expenditures made by Charles' contemporary and kinsman, Louis XIV), but also was the period of the adoption of many new social customs. Among these were a growing addiction to new "foreign" drinks—tea, coffee and chocolate. For the service of these drinks, new silver forms had to be devised and there was an initial floundering of decision in finding the perfect form for each. Chocolate, for instance, was taken quite strong and thick, so that the silver chocolate pots were made with a hole in the lid for the insertion of a stirrer. Figure 40 is an example of a typical early chocolate pot. The pot itself is modeled on a Chinese porcelain vase form, adapted by the addition of a spout and a wooden handle at right angles to it. On the lid is a high circular "chimney" set over a hole for the stirrer. Without these appendages, it will be seen that the pot is a fair translation into silver of a Chinese form, even to the low-domed cover projecting somewhat over the collar of the neck.

The base and shoulder of this object are decorated with alternately convex and concave flutings, swirling in a clockwise direction. Bands of matted work border the fluting, setting off stamped designs of leaves and rosettes. The maker of this chocolate pot was Isaac Dighton, a native London goldsmith who here used the alternating flute design introduced by the numerous and successful Huguenot silversmiths.

The Huguenots had emigrated to London at the end of the seventeenth century, owing to their precarious situation as Protestants in a Catholic country. After 1685, with the repeal of the Edict of Nantes, which had afforded some protection to French Protestants since 1598, the number of French goldsmiths who left their homeland and established themselves in London greatly increased, not entirely to the delight of the indigenous members of the gold-

FIGS. 40, 41   Chocolate pot. London, 1697. Maker: Isaac Dighton. 7¾ in. high. The Metropolitan Museum of Art, New York, Gift of George O. May, 1943.

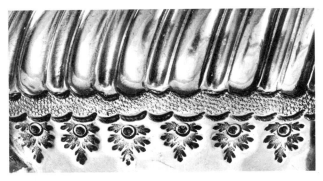

smiths guild. The Frenchmen, however, had much to offer. Although mostly of provincial origin, they had been well trained and brought with them a standard of finesse higher than that required by contemporary taste or even ambition in London. Some styles and decorative techniques that were habitual to them were new to the Londoners.

The helmet-shaped ewer is a typical example of Huguenot work (FRONTISPIECE). It was made by David Willaume and bears the datemark 1700. Willaume came from Metz and was at first supported by the Royal Bounty (as were indeed many other refugee Huguenots and their dependents). In contradistinction to the bold Dutch floral designs and the artless chinoiseries that were the main decorative fare of the period, this ewer, resting in a compact stem and foot and with severely symmetrical ornament, was a return to classic ideas. The cast handle is another classic feature of this particular ewer, both in modeling and conception, for it is none other than a Nereid, a human figure ending in a forked and twining tail, adapted to the function of a handle. Such a figure was lifted wholly from classical antiquity, but it had been a stock motif of European decoration since the Renaissance. A more attenuated example of the same kind of motif, similarly used, forms the handle of the Chinese porcelain ewer already discussed. The base of the ewer now under discussion is handsomely decorated with shells and an arcaded band. This kind of work, called "cut-card" work, one of the earliest features of French silver design favored by the Huguenots, is used for the deeply serrated leaves. Cut-card work was very quickly taken up by the London smiths.

A particularly appealing design in cut-card work appears on a tankard of 1701 made by Joseph Ward (FIG. 42). The term is actually an accurate description, for the design is cut from a flat sheet of silver and soldered to the objects to be decorated. In the case of the tankard illustrated, the cut-cards around the junction of the handle were pierced in a design before being fixed in place, while those on the handle itself are decorated with spines of graduated beading. Cut-card decoration remained popular on one particular vessel—the two-handled covered cup—until the 1740's in England. The applied cards not only had an interesting outer line, but also were very often elaborately decorated within this outline.

FIGS. 42, 43   Tankard. London, 1701. Maker: Joseph
Ward. 8½ in. high. Courtesy the Master and Fellows of
Jesus College, Oxford.

FIG. 44   Teapot. London, 1718. Maker: John Lingard. 6⅛ in. high. The Metropolitan Museum of Art, New York, Rogers Fund, 1913.

V Queen Anne

THE RESTORATION ERA included the reigns of Charles II (1660–1685) and his brother James II (1685–1688). They were succeeded by James's daughter Mary who reigned as co-sovereign with her husband, William, Prince of Orange, who was also her cousin. Their joint reign, the only one in English history, followed the departure of James, who was openly suspected of having converted to Catholicism. He fled London in the so-called "Bloodless Revolution" in 1688. Mary died in 1694 and William in 1702. Mary's younger sister Anne then became queen. Her brief reign (1702–1714) has given its name to a whole style of English decorative art, which, however, insofar as it describes silver wares, germinated before her reign started and certainly lasted for more than a decade after it ended.

Queen Anne silver is marked by an almost total absence of decoration. A combination of causes seems to have united to bring it into being. While great demands were being made on the silversmiths for new wares, there was a scarcity of silver bullion for their use. Dishonest "clippers" made a living for themselves by selling to the silversmiths parcels of silver that had been won by "clipping" pieces of money robbed physically of part of their silver. As the coinage was of the same standard of purity as that required for wrought silver, there was great temptation in the practice of clipping. It was not halted until Parliament at last, as an experiment, ordained that in future, from that date on (1697), the silversmiths were to work with a standard of silver even higher than sterling. The amount of alloy now allowed was only five percent. The amount allowed in sterling was, of course, $7\frac{1}{2}$ percent. The effect of this was that the value of the silver wares increased absolutely, due to the higher grade of silver. Possibly to keep down the cost of such wares, the smiths offered pieces with less actual labor expended in their embellishment. The assay mark on silver while the law was in effect was a figure of Britannia seated with helmet and spear. For this reason silver of the Queen Anne period is often conveniently called "Britannia Standard" ware.

During the same period the lion's-head mark changed from full face to profile and was given a noticeably more shaggy mane. The technical skill needed to cope with the softer metal was certainly not lacking, as the helmet-shaped ewer already discussed and many other large and richly decorated objects from the period abundantly prove. For objects for general sale and regular domestic use, however, the unadorned Queen Anne style represented a perfect accommodation to the new metal. In addition, the faceted forms and carefully proportioned moldings that were its special feature had already been introduced, and could be adapted virtually to every object of domestic plate. Both Huguenot and English smiths worked in this style.

 The candlestick of 1706 by Lewis Mettayer and the teapot of 1718 by John Lingard, both illustrated (FIGS. 57, 44), are organized on an octagonal plan, which in the case of the teapot is carried through the domed lid. Here the appeal of the objects rests solely on the attractiveness of the forms themselves and the different intensities of radiance reflected from their polished surfaces. Candlesticks, though made in the previous centuries, became particularly numerous and popular in the opening years of the eighteenth century and remained a standard object of the silversmiths' general production throughout. Teapots also, though the first one seems to be that of 1670, associated with the East India Company, became an item in steady demand and various patterns, both octagonal and rounded, were devised for them. Tea drinking became general among the fashionable classes, although it was always an expensive habit. Teapots made before 1750 were, on the whole, smaller than those made later, and reflect the cost of tea drinking. The amount of tea taken by an individual at any one sitting was relatively small, as may easily be surmised from the diminutive teabowls used. The teapot by John Lingard holds only 19 fluid ounces, yet probably served four or more.

Simon Pantin was a Huguenot who adapted his styling perfectly to the requirements of the contemporary market. He was apprenticed in London to the French smith Pierre Harache, a native of Rouen. Pantin won a large and fashionable clientele among the nobility and became one of the most famous of the Huguenots working in London. A silver standish of 1725 by Pantin is an interesting continuation of the Queen Anne style. The tray is a generous rectangle rounded at the corners and gently curved from the horizontal to the vertical to provide a restraining edge for the three receptacles on it. The equipment of this standish consists of a bell, an inkpot and a sander. The bell is a standard item on standishes, for these usually were found in one of the living areas of a home—the withdrawing room, or the library or bedroom, definitely not an "office"—and a message having been written, the bell was required to summon a servant immediately to take it on its way. The two containers are straight-sided drum shapes reinforced with slightly outsetting concentric moldings at the top and the bottom. A finely pierced pattern on the top of the sander makes an object of visual delight out of the necessary outlets for the sand, which at the time took the place of blotting paper, not yet invented. French finesse is seen in the delicacy of the leaf forms used for the pierced pattern and its radial organization. Four short feet at the corners of the tray raise it slightly from the plane. The feet are represented as a square section bar tightly c-scrolled at the end to form a sturdy pad. This strong element also derives from French seventeenth-century design and demonstrates the successful adaptation of French classical elements simplified to harmonize with the Queen Anne style (FIG. 38).

Pierced decoration similar to that on the sander was used on vase-shaped pepper and sugar shakers introduced in the Queen Anne period. In the same period a new similarly shaped form was developed for dispensing salt. These relatively tall objects had usually plain or octagonal lower sections and a pierced upper section that was totally removable, held securely in place with bayonet fittings. Sets of three shakers were often made, that for sugar often being somewhat larger than the other two. On the salt, the top was pierced with a fairly large hole, but in order to be in conformity with the other two shakers in the set, which were pierced, a similar pattern was impressed on it "blind" (FIG. 45). The use of the large common salt finally ended in the latter part of the seventeenth century and its place was taken by the trencher salt, a small dish placed beside each individual's plate, or "trencher." This piece had been gaining in popularity for some time before the total cessation of the use of the large common salt. Throughout the eighteenth century the two ways of dispensing salt, from a shaker or from the trencher salt, existed side by side and, indeed, it is still a matter of choice today. Trencher salts acquired many different forms in the eighteenth century, and their decoration changed with fashion. Few, however, were as charming and basic as the one illustrated (FIG. 34), by Thomas Folkingham, datemarked 1714. It consists of an octagonal base faceted and stepped with a shallow well.

Chamber candlesticks were customarily lit at a candle downstairs and carried in the hand to "light one up to bed." Hence their generally short stalk for the candle and the relatively wide drip pan. Though bearing the mark of the Huguenot Augustine Courtauld, there is no trace of French influence in the delightful chamber candlestick illustrated (FIG. 1). It is completely functional, the drip pan being indeed a shallow bowl, but care was taken to make a pleasing effect in the modest moldings at the base of the candle holder and the shaped handle. The three bun feet recall English furniture design of a slightly earlier period and add a sturdy note.

In the Queen Anne period a large number of special pieces for the tea table and the dinner table made their first appearance. Such, for instance, were the single- and double-lipped sauceboats, dinner knives and forks, spoons for dessert with matching decoration, sets of trays and small waiters, soup tureens, large meat dishes, cruets, mustard pots, teakettles (some on high silver stands), tea trays, sugar bowls and creamers, small teaspoons and pierced "mote skimmers." Teapots and coffeepots at first tended to be similar, but the coffeepot soon took on the taller shape, whereas teapots tended to be made in lower and more compact forms, on an octagonal, rounded or pear-shaped plan. The bullet-shaped teapot had a brief vogue and was completely spherical with a finely fitted lid and straight tapering spout. Round and octagonal plates have survived in some numbers and covered dishes also.

The individual silver wine cup had long since been passed over in favor of the wineglass. The establishment under protection of a native glass industry with a unique new glass material, the famous English lead glass, had no doubt hastened its end. The silver tankard for partaking of the more copious draughts of beer and ale remained in favor and actually increased in size. Tankards had always been provided with covers. Those of the eighteenth century usually had flat or stepped covers and straight sides. A beer mug without a cover was also developed in this century, sometimes with a bulbous shape. Beer jugs also made their appearance in the early eighteenth century; the one illustrated (FIG. 47) bears the datemark 1709 and the maker's mark of Seth Lofthouse. It is generous in capacity to match the thirsts indicated by the size of the contemporary tankard. Its necessarily stout handle is hollow and D-shaped in section, made from cut and soldered strips. Only small areas of cut-card work in a leaf-outline ornament this jug around the spout and at the upper and lower points of juncture of the handle. A number of objects from the workshop of Seth Lofthouse and his brother Matthew have survived and demonstrate their mastery of the subtleties of the plain style. A feeling for proportion was an especially valuable part of the silversmiths' ability in a period when very little decoration, or none at all, was used.

Seth and Matthew Lofthouse, as English as their names, were patronized by members of the Oxford colleges as well as by several of the London Livery Companies and official circles of the courts for ambassadorial services and the like. It was the practice to grant newly appointed ambassadors to foreign courts a service of plate to sustain their dignity as the sovereign's representative. Such services ultimately became very large and the practice became an abuse, the silver being regarded as a perquisite of office and not being returned to the Jewel Office (from which the grants were made) at the end of the appointment. The practice was finally discontinued in 1830. It was then forgotten that the pieces in ambassadorial services had been customarily engraved with the royal coat of arms and the initials of the sovereign in whose service the ambassador had set forth (AR, GR and so on). Coming onto the market years later, such pieces were thought to have been the personal or official property of the sovereign, but this was not the case. The Huguenot as well as the London smiths seem to have benefited equally from these orders (FIG. 45).

The important covered cup of vase shape had attained its form in the Restoration period, although, in fact, it was no more than an elongated development of the double-handled covered porringer of the type already illustrated. In the eighteenth century these cups may have been used for drinking on formal occasions. They often also were the prize for certain horse races, as indeed is still the custom, but their general use seems to have become obsolete as the century progressed. Nevertheless it was *de rigueur* for such cups to continue to appear on the sideboard or center of the table in the fashionable dining room, and as decorative objects such cups were often very handsomely embellished. Colleges and other corporate bodies, however, still kept the custom of "passing the loving cup" clockwise around the table at corporate mealtimes or special celebrations, when the two handles were particularly useful for the safe transference of the cup from one pair of hands to the next. The loving cup, like the great salt of an earlier period, was a specifically English form; nevertheless splendid examples were made by the Huguenots and it may even be held that, under their handling, it achieved a new and elegant urn shape with domed lid in several stages. The cup illustrated in Figure 46 is by Simon Pantin and bears the datemark 1709. It is a consummate piece in the Queen Anne style.

Simon Pantin was the master to whom the greatest of the eighteenth-century silversmiths was apprenticed from 1705 to 1712. He was Paul de Lamerie, of French parentage but brought up and trained in England. He no doubt acquired from his master and from the French influences that must have surrounded him as a boy a special appreciation of the finest work. De Lamerie's active career extended from the period of great restraint and plainness to the period of greatest exuberance in English silver. He entered his mark as an independent master in 1712, that is, when the Britannia Standard was in force, and he worked as a silversmith until a few months before his death in 1753. Throughout his career he was the leader in adopting the newest styles and applying them to silver. It is not surprising that he should be particularly conscious of what was new across the channel in France, and the style for which he was to be most famous, the so-called Rococo style, was born there. A double-lipped sauceboat, shown in Figure 49, is an example of his sculptural approach even to so humdrum an object as this. There is no decoration except the applied molding swinging around the midpoint of the boat-shaped vessel in unison with the cut, syncopated edge. This is a foretaste of what de Lamerie would do when the Rococo style was more salable in the next decade.

Above: FIG. 46 Covered cup. London, 1709. Maker: Simon Pantin. 8⅞ in. high. The Metropolitan Museum of Art, New York, Gift of Irwin Untermyer, 1958.

Below: FIG. 47 Beer jug. London, 1709. Maker: Seth Lofthouse. 11⅛ in. high. The Metropolitan Museum of Art, New York, The Jules S. Bache Collection, 1949.

Opposite: FIG. 45 Casters from an ambassadorial service. London, 1710. Maker: Lewis Mettayer. Tallest: 6¾ in. high. Private collection.

FIG. 48   Tureen. London, 1736. Maker: Paul de Lamerie. 12 in. high. The Metropolitan Museum of Art, New York, The Jules S. Bache Collection, 1949.

VI Rococo and Adam

QUEEN ANNE WAS already middle-aged at the time of her accession and none of her numerous children survived her. At her death the throne, by prearrangement of Parliament, passed to the closest Protestant representative of the blood royal. Thus her brother James's Catholic son, Charles Stuart, was passed over in favor of the king of Hanover, who happened to be a great grandson of James I. He came to the throne of England as George I, thus beginning a period of more than a century (1714–1830) when a George sat on the throne of England. In the decorative arts the term "Georgian" is given to the whole period. Since this is such a long period, however, it is best to describe the various silver styles that succeeded one another by some other names than merely Georgian. This term is useful (and not always then) only when applied to the most serviceable of dinner equipment, which changed little in form and was very little decorated. The terms used for the various silver styles are best called "early Rococo," "full Rococo," "exhausted Rococo," and Adam, followed by Regency. This brings us safely to 1820, when George IV came to the throne after serving many years as regent during his father's interesting and ill-diagnosed "indisposition." Such a scheme is preferable to the naming of silver even from the name of each sovereign in turn, George I, George II, etc., for the Queen Anne style was at its height during the reign of the first George and the reign of George III included all the styles from the "exhausted Rococo" to the Regency.

The Rococo was at first an architectural manner used for the decoration of flat wall surfaces in royal interiors in France. It tended at first to be light but symmetrical and combined abstract trellis and other geometrical patterns with vegetable and marine motifs. In English silver this influence was first seen in the 1720's in light flat-chased patterns on simple objects such as small square waiters and salvers, which presented a flat expanse of polished metal on which the design could be displayed. Such patterns were also at first perfectly symmetrical in the essential points of balance and tended to be of masks or profile heads flanked by bands of trellis pattern and herbage. Only a few independent trailing tendrils escaped, as it were, from formal control. De Lamerie was one of the first London silversmiths to offer objects decorated in this manner.

The quietly asymmetrical first Rococo style remained long in fashion, with an evolution of the minor details. A more florid form is seen as the principal decoration of a salver with "pie-crust" border of 1742–1743, probably by John Swift (FIG. 16). The beautifully worked design in the flat part of the salver is composed of strangely assorted elements: shaped panels of trellis, fruit and flower arrangements, large and small shells—none too identifiable from a strictly scientific point of view—human busts in shaped shell-edged reserves and slender fronds of palm. Similar fruit, flowers, shells and palm are grouped also around the central coat of arms (Bray impaling Sadleir) in a free asymmetrical fashion. Asymmetry is not, however, synonymous with imbalance. In terms of visual weight, if one can so describe it, the sum of the decoration to each side of an imaginary vertical dividing line balances the other. Furthermore, the actual form of the salver is a perfectly stable hexagon, every edge of the hexagon being outlined by a c-scroll flanked by s-scrolls. The basic symmetry of the form is successfully disguised by the swirling movement of the scrolls themselves, the larger areas of foam motifs and the smaller of shells. Examination will reveal, however, that even these are rationally and proportionally disposed; where two s-scrolls meet—that is to say, at the angles of

Above left: FIG. 50   Salver. London, 1726. Maker: Paul de Lamerie. 13¼ in.
square. Courtesy S. J. Shrubsole, New York.
Right: FIG. 51   Plate. London, 1746. Maker: Paul de Lamerie. 9⅝ in. diameter.
The Metropolitan Museum of Art, New York, Bequest of Alfred Duane Pell, 1925.
Opposite: FIG. 49   Double-lipped sauceboat. London, 1717. Maker: Paul de La-
merie. 7½ in. wide. The Metropolitan Museum of Art, New York, Gift of George
D. Widener and Eleanor W. Dixon (Mrs. Widener Dixon).

the hexagon—there occur the larger, triangular foam forms; where the other
ends of the s-scrolls meet the c-scrolls at the center of the sides there are
placed the smaller shell forms.

Paul de Lamerie led the way in extending the asymmetrical style into three
dimensions. The tureen of 1736 and the gilt loving cup of 1742 are examples
of the highly ornate Rococo wares for which he was preeminent among the
London goldsmiths. We are dealing with forms such as the salver, which have,
in spite of their heavy asymmetrical decoration in relief, a basic stability
derived from the regularity of the shape itself. The tureen is embellished with
a strange combination of motifs in relief or sculptural form, the latter including lobsters under the handles and scaly sea serpents forming the four feet,
sprays of vine with leaves and bunches of grapes, and a pair of disembodied
eagle wings above the cartouche containing the armorial. The lion on the finial
of the lid is the family crest used in conjunction with armorials and is not
part of de Lamerie's original design. The sprays of dissimilar plants to each
side of the armorial are familiar in their asymmetrical disposition, which is

seen again in the shaped panels of matte work with polished raised borders that swirl clockwise up the wide finial of the lid. Tempering these and all the other nonsymmetrical parts of the decoration are the regular alternation of narrow and broad sections of the body of the tureen, the rectangular panels with cut corners containing bands of latticework against a matte ground, and the shaped concentric molding of the edge of the cover (FIG. 48).

The gilt loving cup is of a type that by the middle of the eighteenth century had become important as a centerpiece but had very little practical usage. Its remote ancestor was the low two-handled cup of the second half of the seventeenth century, which has already been discussed. Acquiring a cover before the end of the 1660's, it had a steady evolution in height and embellishment until it reached a peak with the Rococo covered cups. The form continued to be made, the decoration changing to fit the times, into the early nineteenth century.

The tall cup by de Lamerie (COLOR PLATE 11), like the tureen, has a great deal of cast work set onto its basic form and the shape itself was probably cast and not raised by the hammer. Some of the relief decoration was made with the original casting of the form; some, in higher relief, was soldered on afterward. The main decoration is pictorial, showing a cherub at play in a vineyard in an extremely irregularly shaped panel, which is surrounded with scrolls and leaves, while on the foot is an apparently inebriated lion and peering over the top of the panel a human mask, possibly meant to symbolize Dionysus.

Rococo decoration not only was applied freely to deliberately ornate pieces like the loving cup just described but was easily adapted to decorate all the equipment of the dining room and the tea table—teapots, caddies, sugar bowls and creamers. Even on candlesticks and candelabra the swirling movement in which the motifs were often arranged was carried through to the disposition of the arms. Throughout the eighteenth century, however, regardless of fashion a great many quite undecorated pieces were made, especially those for the dinner table; there have survived many classic Georgian pieces—tureens, plates, entrée dishes, sauceboats, candlesticks and trays—totally undecorated except for a single rope or gadroon border (FIG. 51). The eighteenth century is in fact the period in which our present notions for the classic forms suitable for useful dinner wares first evolved.

Although before the eighteenth century a few outstanding goldsmiths are known by name, or from a surviving body of characteristic work, it is not

Right: FIG. 52 Tea urn. London, 1773. Maker: John Carter. 20¾ in. high. The Metropolitan Museum of Art, New York, Rogers Fund, 1911.

Below: FIG. 53 Teapot. London, 1779. Maker: probably Francis Stamp. 5⅜ in. high. The Metropolitan Museum of Art, New York, Gift of Frances E. Markoe and Stephen C. Markoe, 1943.

until the eighteenth century that a considerable number of the finest artists in the field are known by name and can have numerous examples of their work connected to them. Paul de Lamerie, Charles Kandler and John Edwards, whose most momentous work was in the Rococo style, may be mentioned. Thomas Heming, goldsmith to the king, is another artist whose work is stamped with an individual quality—that of extreme elegance and refinement.

The evolutionary impetus of the Rococo had spent itself by the end of the 1750's, leaving the goldsmith with little in the way of new direction. In the 1760's, the decade preceding the wholesale adoption of the neoclassic Adam style, much silver was decorated in a kind of weak and exhausted Rococo, or more originally with naturally treated flowers. Heming's work in this decade is extremely interesting in its solution to the problem of working without the guidance of a strong contemporary fashion. The beautiful gilt fruit dish illustrated in COLOR PLATE 11 is an example of this. The form is of a generous hammock shape, everted at the edge all the way to the horizontal plane. The body is divided into convex panels, each cut in a curve at the lip and edged with a cast border of gadroons alternating with leaves. The pointed ends are decorated with cast motifs of leaves set between ribs curved out and down to the vertical plane and tightly scrolled at the end. Similar scrolling ribs decorate the armorial cartouche set on the middle panel of each long side. The cartouche is also outlined with cast work reminiscent of the shellwork of the earlier period but symmetrically arranged. The feet and their attachments to the body are also scrolled and covered with vegetable ornament. The matted work on much of the decoration is of the greatest refinement, an inherent quality of the entire object, with its large plain polished areas and serene low line.

The elaborate epergne made its appearance in this decade, offering an alternative to the centerpiece established earlier. They tended to be of many different designs but usually had one large central container for bread surrounded by little baskets for fruit and sweetmeats. Thomas Powell was a specialist in this kind of object, and many of his epergnes are known today. The one illustrated (FIG. 54), however, is by Thomas Heming and shows quite a different approach to that of the fruit dish just described. The main basket is raised high on a shaped hollow pedestal, which is supported on an openwork base resting on four scroll legs with diamond-shaped feet. From the base four tall pillars, suggestive of palm-tree trunks, support a latticework canopy over the central basket. The canopy is surmounted by a very realistic pineapple. Eight shaped branches also rise from the base, alternately long and short. From the long branches little baskets hang by their handles. The short branches support shallower bowls from underneath. The hollow pineapple in thin silver was presumably made by soldering embossed sections together; the canopy and baskets were hand-raised, then pierced with a saw-cut design, and all the rest of the structural and decorative elements of this generous object were made by casting.

Although its overall size is considerable, being 24½ inches in height and having a spread of 30 inches, the disposition of the epergne's parts spare it from any suggestion of heaviness. There is ample space between the basket and its high canopy, and the pierced decoration of the surrounding baskets, the pedestal, the stand and the canopy also give a suggestion of lightness, while the flowers and leaves that appear profusely on all parts contribute a note of gaiety to the general impression. Pierced work had been very generally used for larger baskets for bread and cake since the 1730's. The epergne of the 1760's saw its extension to other forms, but with similar decorative and practical effect (that of ventilation).

Lightness but not gaiety was the pervading impression of the Neoclassic style, which started to affect the design of silver about 1770 and very quickly became general. Robert Adam, who introduced the style in England, was an architect who designed not only the interiors of the rooms of his houses but also the movable furnishings that went into them, so that the general effect would be one of unity. He is not known to have designed much silver for specific commissions, but the London goldsmiths were able to devise shapes that gave the right suggestion of classic repose and authentic classic ornament to go with the Adamesque interiors that came into vogue. For ornament, indeed, the silversmiths had only to turn the pages of two important archeological books that were illustrated with engraved plates: Robert Wood's *The Ruins of Palmyra,* published in 1753, and *The Ruins of Baalbec,* published in 1757, by the same author.

The tall urn shape was paramount and was used as the basic form for such different items of hollow ware as coffeepots, cream pails, loving cups and tea urns. The tea urn illustrated (FIG. 52) is datemarked 1773 and bears the mark of John Carter. A square pedestal on four paw feet is jointed to the fluted stem of the urn, which has a half-round edge. Similar fluting decorates the lower part of the body and that part of it above the shoulder where it rises steeply and narrows to a small vertical neck having a domed cover. Two lion masks and two satyr masks are set alternately around the shoulder with swags of drapery hanging between them. This rather severe object is very much in contrast to urns of the previous decade, which often manage, in spite of the difficulty of the form, to appear rather playful. The urn shape was also used in a lower form for smaller objects such as sugar bowls, which were often pierced in designs of the prevailing taste.

The urn shape itself was often used as a decorative motif, as is seen, for instance, in the rim of the salver illustrated on page 29. The salver is plain, except for the arms of the Bacon family engraved in the center in a handsome frame. The edge is slightly raised and vertically pierced, while a band of wave pattern decorates the perimeter. Upon the pierced edge are set alternately little urns and paterae (small stylized flower heads) joined by swags of laurel. In this period other classic ornaments—ram heads, running key patterns bound by leaves, husk festoons and acanthus leaves—were also used, but sparingly and always rather widely spaced, giving a sense of clarity quite different from the massed-together use of similar motifs favored earlier, in the Tudor period.

Mechanical methods had by now taken over certain processes formerly done by hand, such as preparing sheets of silver. Rolling presses could now do this very quickly and in a variety of gauges; the silversmith could buy his material in sheet form and devise methods to take advantage of this. Cutting and seaming had been used as early as the Elizabethan age to make straight-sided beakers. Now other wares using the same method were promoted.

The teapot illustrated (FIG. 53) is a good example. The oval bottom and top are cut from sheet metal, and the side walls also cut out and seamed vertically, then soldered to the base and top. This was economical in time and metal and resulted in an article that could be bought by a middle class of increased spending power that had gradually grown up in the eighteenth century. Many charming and modest tea services were made for this class. To ornament the lighter metal, a new form of decorative work called "bright cutting" was invented. By this method, design, usually of a linear nature, could be carried out by literally slicing off small areas of the surface of the metal with a sharp hand tool. The result was a series of tiny sparkling facets. Such an effect was quite in keeping with the contemporary faceted crystal and cut-steel accessories that were also to be seen in domestic interiors. A kind of

tea caddy often made in sets of two or three that could be fabricated successfully from the rolled silver sheets was represented as a tea chest—of the kind
that tea was shipped in from the East in bulk. Sometimes a large and decorative Chinese character was engraved on the lid or the sides to enforce the
suggestion; sometimes an engraved floral pattern suggestive of textile cover-
ing was added.

FIG. 54   Epergne. London, 1766. Maker: Thomas Heming. 24½ in. high. The
Metropolitan Museum of Art, New York, Gift of Lewis Einstein, 1952.

FIG. 55 Fruit basket. London, 1814. Maker: Paul Storr. 13¾ in. high. The Metropolitan Museum of Art, New York, Gift of Mrs. Chester Hamilton Lehman, 1965.

VII Regency

THE LIGHTNESS BOTH of the pieces made strictly in the fashionable Adam taste and of those other domestic objects made for the larger silver-buying public that was not so likely to require styles in the latest fad of St. James, was subdued by the heavy classicism of the next period—that known as the Regency. As early as 1799 a book by Charles Heathcote Tatham, *Ancient Ornamental Architecture at Rome and Italy,* was published giving his preference for the denser aspects of Roman design. Classic ornament in the earlier Adam period had been taken from the eastern Mediterranean and Greek models. Tatham made his ideas explicit in 1806 with the publication of *Designs for Ornamental Plate,* in which he said, "Instead of *Massiveness,* the principle characteristic of good plate, light and insignificant forms have prevailed to the utter exclusion of all good ornament whatsoever." A leaning to massiveness was indeed one of the strands of taste in the Regency period, and the one that had the most pronounced effect on silver design, though it should not be forgotten that in architecture and interiors, fantasy was also appreciated and led to the creation of Gothic, Oriental and Egyptian atmospheres.

The covered sugar bowl (FIG. 56) certainly satisfies the requirement of "massiveness" and "good ornament" advocated by Tatham. It is not part of a tea set but a large (8 inches high) solitary reservoir for sugar meant for the dining table. Its shape is modeled on a Roman urn. It stands on a small foot, rising briefly into a constricted stem on which the bulbous body is immediately set. This narrows at the lip and is surmounted by a low-domed cover in two stages. The most prominent decoration is the wide band of scrolled ornament around the broadest part of the bowl. This was of classical origin and appeared very frequently on silver in the Adam period but usually on a much smaller and daintier scale. Here, by increasing the size of the decorative motif very much, in relation to the area to be decorated (nine repeats suffice to encircle the bowl, where many more would be required for the same distance in the Adam period), an air of weight and solemnity is achieved. The bowl stands on a plateau raised on four round feet partly concealed by triangular brackets decorated with a type of anthemion motif. The sugar bowl is dated 1814 and bears the mark of the partners Benjamin and James Smith. They made a great deal of "massive" plate during the Regency, much of it to the order of the overbusy firm of Rundell, Bridge and Rundell, which received many commissions from the Regent himself.

Benjamin and James Smith, Digby Scott, Rundell, Bridge and Rundell, and Paul Storr were the leaders of the London silversmiths in the production of stylishly heavy, massively conceived silver. Their operations were more in the nature of commercial partnerships of masters employing a very large number of workmen rather than a master with a small group of journeymen and apprentices about him, as had been customary in earlier centuries.

The sugar bowl discussed above was part of the service of plate allowed to the Duke of Wellington on his appointment in 1814 as ambassador to Louis XVIII. The practice of equipping ambassadors with a service of plate at the expense of the Jewel Office (at state expense, so to speak) has already been described. Wellington's was probably one of the last posts to be fitted out in this way before the custom was abolished. The service was made up by purchases from the open stock of the London shops, rather than a specially designed service. Wellington himself had earlier received one so designed in 1806 and in fact was the recipient of a great deal of silver in the form of special presentations.

 The fruit basket by Paul Storr illustrated in Figure 55 is very similar to those in the Wellington ambassadorial service. The basket itself is of plaited wirework with a wide border of cast vine leaves against an *ajouré* ground. At the base of the basket is a band of shell and anthemion ornament, a frieze design that, like the running floral scroll on the sugar bowl, was first used on English silver in the Adam period, although it stemmed directly from classical architecture. Architectonic also is the concept of raising the basket on the heads of three maidens in classical dress who support between them crossed thyrsi tied with ribbons. This classic wand was the attribute of Dionysus (the god of wine), maenads and bacchantes, and presumably was deliberately included to refer again to the grapes which the fruit basket probably was intended to hold. The base consists of a triangular plinth raised on three bracket-shaped feet in the form of satyr masks that rest on a second triangular plinth supported on three vertical feet similar to those on the fruit basket.

After the Regency, the styles of the nineteenth century tended to become more confused in their combination of decorative motifs from a variety of sources and periods, including styles of earlier English silver wares. Commercial competition from Birmingham and Sheffield was keenly felt, and a great deal of mechanization was adopted for processes earlier done by hand. The abolition of the Apprenticeship Act in 1814 meant that manufacturers of silver did not necessarily need any training in the traditional hand techniques. Inevitably, mechanization led to mass production and the disappearance of the independent silversmith. Therefore, 1820 is a suitable point at which to close this review of London-made silver from late Tudor to Regency times.

FIG. 56   Sugar bowl. London, 1814. Makers: Benjamin and James Smith. 8 in. high. Victoria and Albert Museum, London.

General Survey

HEAL, SIR AMBROSE, F.S.A. *The London Goldsmiths 1200-1800. A record of the names and addresses of the craftsmen, their shopsigns and trade cards.* Cambridge, 1935.

HUGHES, BERNARD and THERLE. *Three Centuries of English Domestic Silver.* London, 1952.

JONES, E. ALFRED. *Old Silver of Europe and America.* Philadelphia, 1928.

OMAN, C. C. *English Domestic Silver.* London, 1934.

TAYLOR, GERALD. *Silver.* Baltimore, 1963.

Hallmarks

JACKSON, SIR CHARLES J. *English Goldsmiths and Their Marks.* London, 1921, and New York, 1964.

Special Subjects

GASK, N. *Old Silver Spoons of England.* London, 1926.

HAYWARD, J. F. *Huguenot Silver in England 1688-1727.* London, 1959.

How, G. E. P. and J. P. *English and Scottish Silver Spoons.* 3 Vols., London, 1952-1957.

OMAN, C. C. *English Church Plate 597-1830.* London, 1957.

——. *The English Silver in the Kremlin 1557-1663.* London, 1961.

ROWE, ROBERT. *Adam Silver 1765-1795.* London, 1965.

RUPERT, C. G. *Apostle Spoons.* Oxford, 1929.

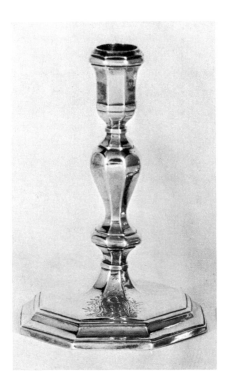

FIG. 57 Candlestick. London, 1706. Maker: Lewis Mettayer. 6⅝ in. high. The Metropolitan Museum of Art, New York, Bequest of Mary Strong Shattuck, 1935.